Sex hidden in the PULPIT

RESTORING INTEGRITY & REBUILDING TRUST IN CHURCH LEADERSHIP

Monsenaray Sheppard

Sex Hidden in the Pulpit
Restoring Integrity & Rebuilding Trust in Church Leadership
Copyright © 2024 Monsenaray Sheppard

The scanning, uploading, reproduction, and distribution of this book, in any form, stored in a retrieval system, or transmitted in any form by any means—electric, mechanical, photocopy, recording, or otherwise—without prior written permission of the author, except as provided by United States of America copyright law, is a theft of the author's intellectual property. If you would like permission to use materials from the book (other than for a review), please contact the author.

Thank you for your support of the author's rights.

All Scripture quotations are from the King James Version (KJV), unless otherwise noted. Scripture taken from the New King James Version®. Copyright © 1982 by Thomas Nelson. Used by permission. All rights reserved. Scripture quotations marked (NIV) are taken from the Holy Bible, New International Version®, NIV®. Copyright © 1973, 1978, 1984, 2011 by Biblica, Inc.® Used by permission. All rights reserved worldwide. Scripture quotations marked (ESV) are from The ESV® Bible (The Holy Bible, English Standard Version®), copyright © 2001 by Crossway, a publishing ministry of Good News Publishers. Used by permission. All rights reserved.

Book Completion Services Provided by:
TRU Statement Publications—Independent Publishing Made Easy
www.trustatementpublications.com

First Edition: December 2024
Printed in the United States of America
All Rights Reserved
0 0 1 2 0 1 8 2 0 2 4 0 0
ISBN: 9798302462275

Sex hidden in the PULPIT

RESTORING INTEGRITY & REBUILDING TRUST IN CHURCH LEADERSHIP

Monsenaray Sheppard

CONTENTS

Meet The Author Monsenaray Sheppard 1

Introduction: A Call to Restore and Rebuild 3

CH 1: The Battle for Integrity in Leadership 7

CH 2: A Church with a Mission! What Does It Look Like? 15

CH 3: Church, Sex, and the Public 25

CH 4: What Are We as Leaders Doing About the Issue? 35

CH 5: Discipleship for The Unchurched 45

CH 6: Ways to Overcome Sexual Sin 55

CH 7: Breaking Free Through Christ 65

Meet the Author:
MONSENARAY SHEPPARD

"Only what we do for Christ will last, and it is my prayer that this work inspires the church to rise to its calling with integrity, love, and accountability."

Evangelist Monsenaray Sheppard is a woman of faith, integrity, and a passion for the church's mission to reflect God's love, holiness, and truth. Born in Muskegon, Michigan, on May 10, 1958, her journey in ministry began when she was baptized in the name of Jesus at the young age of 11 under the leadership of Bishop Burrell in Muskegon. Though her spiritual walk began early, it wasn't until she was 32 years old that she received the gift of the Holy Ghost—an experience that transformed her life and solidified her calling to serve.

After moving to Flint, Michigan, and later to Lawton, Oklahoma, Evangelist Sheppard answered the call to ministry under the guidance of Suffragan Bishop Joseph Readen. Her leadership and dedication have been evident throughout her service in various capacities within the Pentecostal Assemblies of the World (P.A.W.). She has served as a missionary director, chaplain, and state-level leader in the Missionary Auxiliary, where she demonstrated a heart for equipping and uplifting others in their faith journeys. Her approach to leadership has always been marked by humility, choosing to focus on God's purpose over personal recognition, as reflected in one of her favorite quotes: *"Much can be accomplished if we don't mind who gets the credit."*

Evangelist Sheppard is a lifelong learner, committed to deepening her understanding of God's Word and its application to ministry. In her 40s, she earned an undergraduate degree in Health Care Administration, followed by a Master's in Religious Studies with an equivalency in Master of Divinity (MDiv). She is now pursuing a Doctorate in Ministry, specializing in chaplaincy, where she continues to focus on helping people from all walks of life find hope and transformation through Christ.

Currently residing in Conyers, Georgia, Evangelist Sheppard serves faithfully under the leadership of Pastor Stewart Reese III and Lady Wanda Reese. Her greatest desire is to see lives changed for the better, no matter their background. She firmly believes that only what we do for Christ will last, and her ministry reflects this truth in both word and action. She is inspired daily by the scripture: *"Having obtained help from the Lord, I continue unto this day"* (Acts 26:22).

As the author of this book, Evangelist Monsenaray Sheppard brings a clarion call to the church and its leaders. Her years of experience in ministry, her academic preparation, and her heartfelt desire to see the church restored to a place of holiness and trust make her a credible and reputable voice to address this pressing issue. With humility and boldness, she challenges the body of Christ to confront difficult truths, embrace accountability, and pursue lasting change.

Introduction
A CALL TO RESTORE AND REBUILD

"The church cannot heal if we are unwilling to confront the very issues that threaten its foundation. Restoring integrity and rebuilding trust is not just the responsibility of leadership—it's a collective calling for every believer."

The church, the body of Christ, is a sacred place—meant to be a sanctuary of love, healing, and truth. Yet, we are facing an issue that strikes at the very heart of this calling: sexual sin within church leadership. It's a subject that many would prefer to avoid, but one that is silently tearing apart the fabric of trust and integrity upon which the church was built.

I didn't choose to write this book because it's easy. I chose to write it because it's necessary. Sexual sin in leadership is an issue that has been swept under the rug for far too long. The damage it causes ripples through entire congregations, leaving behind broken trust, wounded hearts, and disillusioned believers. But, more than that, it has the potential to sever the connection between the church and the very people it is called to serve. The world is watching, and when we, as the body of Christ, fail to uphold the standards of holiness and accountability, it leaves lasting scars on the witness of the church.

Maybe you've experienced this issue firsthand. Maybe you've seen the fallout when a pastor or leader's moral failure is exposed. Or perhaps you haven't encountered this struggle directly, but you still feel a sense of urgency for the church to return to the integrity and trust that should define it. This book is for all of us—for those who have been affected, for those who feel called to be part of the solution, and for every believer who longs to see the church thrive in its mission once again.

This isn't about pointing fingers or casting judgment. It's about healing. It's about finding a way forward, together. As members of the body of Christ, we are all called to uphold one another in love, to restore those who have fallen, and to rebuild trust where it has been broken. Restoring integrity to the church's leadership is not just the responsibility of those in authority; it is a collective responsibility. The church cannot heal if we are unwilling to confront the very issues that threaten its foundation.

Throughout this book, we will delve into the realities of sexual sin in leadership, not to sensationalize or shame, but to expose the root causes and offer real biblical solutions. We will explore how this issue has damaged the church's witness, why it persists, and, most importantly, how we can restore what has been lost. This journey is not just about addressing one type of sin; it is about rebuilding a culture of accountability, transparency, and grace within the church.

For those who have been hurt or disillusioned, my prayer is that this book will offer a path to healing and hope. For those who lead, may it serve as a reminder that the call to ministry is a sacred trust, one that requires constant vigilance and humility. And for every reader, my deepest hope is that you will not turn away from this issue, but rather, lean into the challenge of helping the church recover its integrity and rebuild its trust.

No matter where you stand—whether as a leader, a congregant, or someone watching from the outside—this is your invitation to be part of the solution. The church needs people willing to stand in the gap, to restore what's broken, and to rebuild what's been lost. Together, we can create a future where the church once again stands as a beacon of hope, truth, and love.

The time for healing is now. Let's begin.

Chapter 1
THE BATTLE FOR INTEGRITY IN LEADERSHIP

"Victory over sexual sin is not a one-time event; it is a daily battle requiring honesty, accountability, and reliance on God's grace. Temptation will come, but through Christ, we have the power to overcome."

Sexual sin is a deeply rooted struggle that many face, and leaders in the church are not exempt from this battle. While overcoming such behavior is possible, the question often arises: Will temptation cease once the sin is conquered? The answer is no. Temptation does not disappear, and it is certain that it will resurface time and again. However, the promise of God is greater than any temptation.

"There hath no temptation taken hold of you but such as is common to man. But God is faithful: He will not suffer you to be tempted beyond that which ye are able to bear, but with the temptation will also make a way to escape, that ye may be able to bear it" (1 Corinthians 10:13).

Layers of Sin and False Intimacy

Sexual sin comes in many forms and layers, and overcoming it requires both desire and commitment to a life that pleases

God. One recurring question is: Why do people fall into sexual sin? This struggle is not limited to men; women, too, especially those in leadership, find themselves entangled in ungodly affairs. False intimacy is a common thread in these situations—a counterfeit form of connection that only leads to deeper entanglement in sin.

Many who battle these behaviors often feel hopeless, as though they can never overcome. The reality is sexual sin is a persistent temptation. The enemy studies our weaknesses, waiting for the right moment to exploit them. But victory is possible through Christ, though it requires constant vigilance and spiritual strength.

What Does It Mean to Overcome?

The word nikao in the Bible, meaning "to overcome," speaks of subduing, conquering, or gaining victory. It's important to understand that overcoming sin is not a passive event—it requires fighting and striving for victory. It is a battle, and victories often come with a price. There is no easy road to overcoming, especially in matters of sexual sin.

Personal Testimony: My Journey of Struggle and Growth

I remember when I first received the Holy Ghost. I was in a relationship with a boyfriend of eight years, and despite my newfound faith, I still craved him physically. I struggled with my flesh, often falling back into old behaviors. Confession was encouraged, so I went to my pastor, Bishop Willie Burrel, in my hometown of Muskegon, Michigan. He would pray for me, and I believed I was restored. Yet, the behavior persisted.

After years of this cycle, I decided to end the relationship because he didn't want to be saved. At the time, I thought I was doing the right thing. I was taught that if someone isn't willing to marry or be saved, it's time to move on. That's exactly what I did. But looking back, I realized that simply removing myself from the relationship didn't address the deeper issue. The craving for intimacy without commitment was still there.

Leaders in Crisis: Where is the Accountability?

Today, we see more leaders than ever succumbing to sexual sin. Where are the pastors who will hold us accountable, like those in the past? The modern church is facing a crisis of integrity among its leaders. We often misquote Scripture, saying, "It is better to marry than to burn," and use this as an excuse to enter into marriages for the wrong reasons.

After ending my previous relationship, I moved to Oklahoma, where I met a man who showed interest in God. We got married, and I believed that being married would allow me to have sex and still remain in good standing with the church. However, he wasn't saved at the time. Eventually, he did get saved and even entered ministry—but not for God, but for me. A marriage based on superficial reasons will crumble, and after twelve years, ours ended.

Covering Sin with a Band-Aid

I found myself back in familiar patterns. Was I ever really delivered, or had I just used marriage as a cover for my behavior? Many leaders fall into this trap—acting as if they're living a life pleasing to God while harboring secret sins. God cannot get the glory from a life lived in hypocrisy. I had to confront my own heart and admit that I needed real healing.

Seeking True Deliverance

Until leaders are honest with themselves and with God, there can be no healing. We must come to a point where we say, "It's me, God. I need help." Sexual maturity and spiritual maturity go hand in hand, and both are necessary for true deliverance.

A Promise of Redemption and Restoration

There is hope for those who have been damaged by sexual sin. David, too, struggled with his flesh and found himself in sinful situations, but he cried out to God for mercy. In Psalm 51:1-4, David pleads for God's forgiveness and restoration. He recognized his sin and sought God's cleansing.

"Have mercy upon me, O God, according to thy lovingkindness: according unto the multitude of thy tender mercies blot out my transgressions. Wash me thoroughly from mine iniquity and cleanse me from my sin. For I acknowledge my transgressions: and my sin is ever before me. Against thee, thee only, have I sinned, and done this evil in thy sight."

As leaders, we must take ownership of our sins. We shouldn't wait to be sat down or disciplined when we fall out of line with God's word. We should have enough integrity to step down voluntarily and seek restoration.

Reflection | Action | Prayer

This reflection section is designed to help you take an honest look at the areas in your life where you may be struggling with temptation or sin. As you answer the questions, allow the Holy Spirit to reveal areas where you need healing and strength.

Take time to engage in the action steps, such as prayer and accountability, knowing that you don't have to face these battles alone. End with a prayer, asking for God's help to overcome sin and walk in His strength.

Reflection Questions:

1. Are there areas in my life where I am struggling to overcome temptation?

_____
_____
_____
_____
_____
_____
_____
_____

2. Do I truly believe that God has given me the strength to resist temptation, or do I feel powerless?

_____
_____
_____
_____
_____
_____
_____
_____

How can I take the first step toward accountability and confession of hidden sins in my life?

_____
_____
_____
_____
_____
_____
_____
_____

3. What does victory over sin look like for me personally?

_____
_____
_____
_____
_____
_____
_____
_____

Future Action Steps:

- Identify someone trustworthy with whom you can share any hidden struggles and seek their support.

- Read and meditate on 1 Corinthians 10:13, reflecting on God's faithfulness in providing a way out of temptation.

- Set aside time each day to pray specifically for strength to resist temptation.

A Prayer for Strength and Victory Over Temptation

Heavenly Father, I come before You with a heart of repentance, acknowledging my weakness in the face of temptation. I thank You for Your promise in 1 Corinthians 10:13, that no temptation has overtaken me except what is common to mankind, and that You will always provide a way out.

I declare that through Christ, I have the power to overcome sin and live a life pleasing to You. Help me to walk in the Spirit, so I do not gratify the desires of the flesh (Galatians 5:16). Renew my mind and transform my heart, as I commit myself to live in Your truth. In Jesus' name, Amen.

Chapter 2
A CHURCH WITH A MISSION! WHAT DOES IT LOOK LIKE?

"A church with a mission reflects the love of Christ, upholds the gospel, and stands firm in holiness—shining as a light in a world longing for truth."

A church with a mission is a church with purpose, integrity, and a clear sense of responsibility to both its members and the world. Congregations that are truly missional embody four essential traits: they are eschatological, creational, sacramental, and incarnational. These traits form the foundation of a church dedicated to advancing God's kingdom. But in today's world, many churches have strayed from these core principles.

The Mission of the Church

The missional church is called to share the gospel with every nation, creating disciples and leading individuals to respond in faith and repentance. This mission reflects the power of the Spirit working in the church. Unfortunately, the biblical texts that once guided our understanding of the church's global mission have become disconnected from the daily lives of many congregations. In the 21st century, many churches no longer preach or teach these foundational truths.

Leaders must recognize that revitalizing the church requires a return to the basics: loving one another and preaching the gospel in its purest form. The church's mission goes beyond spiritual matters; it must also promote the welfare of the community, evangelize, and compassionately meet human needs.

Understanding Jesus' Mission

From the beginning of creation, God has established a relationship with humanity. In the person of Jesus Christ, God became human to atone for our sins and restore our relationship with Him. The Gospel of John illustrates this beautifully. John introduces Jesus to the world, explaining that Jesus is the ultimate expression of God's love: *"For God so loved the world, that He gave His only begotten Son"* (John 3:16).

John's gospel is often referred to as the Gospel of Love because it invites people into a transformative encounter with God through Jesus Christ. It's a gospel that calls believers to love one another as Christ has loved us. This love is not passive—it is active, incarnational, and sacrificial. The mission of the church must reflect this same love, drawing people in, equipping them, and sending them out to share the good news.

Restoring Integrity and Rebuilding Trust in Church Leadership

A Church in Crisis: Addressing Leadership Failures

While the church is called to be a beacon of hope and love, many leaders have fallen into sinful behaviors that damage both the church and the individuals within it. Sexual immorality among church leaders has become a persistent issue, and it is too often ignored or mishandled. When leaders engage in unethical behavior—whether it's adultery, abuse, or inappropriate relationships—the church suffers.

The Bible is clear: *"He who commits adultery lacks sense; he destroys himself"* (Proverbs 6:32 ESV). Yet, despite the severity of this sin, many pastors and leaders continue to function in their roles without facing discipline. This lack of accountability has weakened the church's growth and effectiveness. We have lost sight of what God has called the church to do.

How Should the Church Respond?

It is not enough to simply acknowledge the problem. The church must take action. Leaders who fall into sexual sin must be held accountable, but they also need support and opportunities for restoration. Programs such as *Understanding Clergy and Sexual Ethics* and *Maintaining Boundaries in a Digital Age* offer guidance for leaders who struggle with these issues.

Yet, many churches are afraid to address sexual sin openly for fear of division or losing members. This fear has allowed sinful behaviors to persist unchecked, tarnishing the church's reputation and effectiveness. Instead of ignoring the problem or covering it up, we must confront it with love and grace. As the Bible says, *"We are our brother's keeper."*

There are ways to address these issues without dividing the church. Leaders can be embraced with love while still being held accountable. The goal is not to shame but to help them find healing and restoration.

The Church in Corinth: A Lesson for Today

The church at Corinth faced a similar struggle. Situated in a sexually charged culture, the Corinthian church was surrounded by immorality, yet God's standard remained: *"Be ye holy, for I am holy"* (Leviticus 11:44). The Corinthian church struggled to stand firm against the influences of the world around them. Similarly, today's church must resist the temptation to conform to a culture of moral compromise.

Sexual sin is not a new issue, but its prevalence in church leadership today is alarming. The world has taken what God intended for the sacred covenant of marriage and twisted it into an act of immorality. This distortion of God's gift has infiltrated the church, leading many leaders astray.

Sexual Sin in Leadership: A Call for Integrity

Sexual sin in leadership doesn't only affect the individuals involved—it damages the entire church. When leaders violate their sacred responsibilities, they exploit the trust placed in them by their congregation. This betrayal of trust can cause irreparable harm to the victims, the congregation, and the community.

Pastors who engage in these behaviors often do so repeatedly unless they are confronted and disciplined. These individuals take advantage of their authority and manipulate vulnerable people into inappropriate relationships. This kind of abuse is not only sinful—it is a violation of the pastoral role and a betrayal of God's calling.

The Role of Discipline and Restoration

While the Bible tells us not to judge, it also instructs us to hold each other accountable. *"Purge the evil person from among you,"* says 1 Corinthians 5. This does not mean we should cast out every person who has sinned. Rather, it is a call for church discipline—a process that includes accountability, repentance, and restoration.

Churches that ignore sexual sin are complicit in allowing it to continue. Conversely, churches that offer no grace or path to restoration are missing the mark. The right course of action lies in the balance between discipline and grace. Leaders who fall must be given an opportunity to repent and be restored, but they must also face the consequences of their actions.

The church is called to be holy, set apart from the world. Sexual sin among church leaders is a serious issue that must be addressed with both love and accountability. As we work to restore fallen leaders, we must also protect the integrity of the church and its mission. A church with a mission is one that strives for holiness, upholds the gospel, and reflects the love of Christ in all that it does.

Reflection | Action | Prayer

In this reflection, you are invited to consider how you can personally contribute to the church's mission of sharing the gospel and living with integrity. The questions will challenge you to assess your role in upholding the church's values and calling.

As you reflect, think about practical ways you can be a light in your community and strengthen the church's mission. Use the prayer to ask for God's guidance in living out your faith with purpose and love.

Reflection Questions:

1. Am I contributing to the mission of the church, or am I merely observing from the sidelines?

2. How can I make an impact on my community by sharing the gospel and living as an example of Christ's love?

3. In what areas of my life am I struggling with sin that may affect my witness to others?

Future Action Steps:

- Reflect on how you can actively serve your church's mission and identify one way to get involved in outreach or evangelism.

- Meditate on Matthew 28:19-20 (The Great Commission) and ask God how you can personally fulfill this mission.

- If there is sin in your life, confess it to God and seek guidance from a spiritual leader on how to move forward.

A Prayer for Renewed Commitment to the Church's Mission

Lord, I ask You to reignite my heart with a passion for Your mission, as You have called us to go and make disciples of all nations (Matthew 28:19).

Strengthen my desire to serve Your church with integrity and love, knowing that my labor is not in vain (1 Corinthians 15:58).

Help me, as part of the body of Christ, to love others deeply and to be a reflection of Your truth. May the church return to its foundation in Your Word, and may we shine as lights in a dark world (Matthew 5:14-16). In Jesus' name, Amen.

Chapter 3
CHURCH, SEX, AND THE PUBLIC

"The church's witness to the world is built on transparency, integrity, and humility. To lead others to Christ, we must first reflect His love and grace in all we do."

Jesus called us to be "Fishers of Men," to love one another as He loved us. *"Love thy neighbor as you love yourself,"* He commanded. But here lies the problem: We cannot give what we do not have. In order to give love, we must first love ourselves. The truth is, *"hurt people hurt people."* When leaders in the church struggle with their own unresolved issues, it manifests in their behavior, hurting those they are meant to lead and care for.

Today, many people are searching for a church that preaches biblical truth and maintains a clear moral stance. They're asking, *"Where can I find a church that still teaches that right is right and wrong is wrong?"* Increasingly, churches are changing their message to align with popular culture, focusing on consumerism and a "your best life now" theology. The power of the Holy Spirit is being replaced by emotional manipulation—loud music, flashy presentations, and programs that mirror the world.

But the message of the Bible does not change. Even as culture demands that we call "good" what the Bible calls evil, the truth remains. People are searching for authenticity. They want leaders who live what they preach, especially in matters of sexual integrity.

The Impact of Leadership Failure on the Church

When sexual sin occurs in leadership, it causes deep wounds. Members feel betrayed when they discover that a trusted leader has been involved in immoral behavior. This betrayal often leads to people leaving the church, disillusioned and hurt. The pain is compounded when the pastor or church leadership is aware of the behavior and does nothing to address it. Failing to discipline leaders who engage in such behavior devastates the congregation and erodes trust.

Sexual sin may be permissible between consenting adults, but when boundaries are crossed, it becomes a violation. Scripture is clear about the place of sexuality: it is meant to be enjoyed within the confines of marriage. Outside of that, it leads to destruction. In the book of Revelation, Jesus rebuked churches for their involvement in sexual sin. Paul also spoke to this issue in 1 Corinthians 6:13-14 ESV, saying, *"The body is not meant for sexual immorality, but for the Lord, and the Lord for the body."*

Why Do Leaders Keep Returning to Sexual Sin?

Sexual sin is not just a moral failing—it's often a deep spiritual issue. Many leaders fall into this behavior because they are spiritually dead, lacking the power to overcome temptation. Sexual sin carries a stigma, making it a difficult topic to address openly. It includes a wide range of behaviors—adultery, fornication, homosexuality, lust, and more. These are sins often hidden in secret, giving temptation a foothold. As Proverbs 28:13 says, *"He that covers his sins shall not prosper: but whoso confesses and forsakes them shall have mercy."*

Many make excuses for their behavior rather than take responsibility for it. This avoidance only leads to a deeper entanglement in sin.

Restoration & Accountability: Learning from Fallen Pastors

Ray Carroll, a former pastor, wrote about his experience of marital infidelity and the search for restoration in his book *Fallen Pastors: Finding Restoration in a Broken World*. His research revealed that sexual sin among church leaders is alarmingly common. Carroll's goal is to help spiritual leaders proactively seek to prevent moral failure before it happens. After all, when a leader falls, the consequences ripple beyond their family, affecting their ministry and congregation.

According to Leadership Magazine, a survey of 300 pastors revealed that 41% admitted to marital infidelity. This mirrors the general population, where 20-25% of married individuals admit to engaging in extramarital affairs. The issue of sexual sin is not confined to the church but is a widespread problem. However, its impact is felt more deeply within the church because of the moral and spiritual authority entrusted to its leaders.

Harry Schaumburg, author of *False Intimacy: Understanding the Struggle of Sexual Addiction,* has spent over 30 years helping leaders find restored intimacy with God. His workshops are filled with pastors and missionaries struggling with sexual sin. This is not just a problem—it is a crisis.

The Church's Role in Restoring Leaders

The church's response to sexual sin should be grounded in love and restoration. Galatians 6:1 reminds us, *"Brethren, if a man is overtaken in a fault, ye which are spiritual, restore such a one in the spirit of meekness; considering thyself, lest thou also be tempted."* Our goal should be to restore those who have fallen, not to condemn them. The process of restoration must begin with confession and repentance, followed by a commitment to spiritual growth.

Leaders who fall into sin must be given an opportunity to turn back to God and be restored to their rightful place in the church. However, this does not mean ignoring the seriousness of their actions. Adultery and other forms of sexual sin destroy trust, and it takes time and accountability to rebuild that trust.

The Church's Response to Sexuality and Leadership

Different denominations and traditions have varied perspectives on sexuality and leadership. Some churches, particularly liberal ones, believe that sex is God's gift and can be enjoyed outside of marriage. However, God's standard is clear: sexual relations are meant to be reserved for marriage. When leaders violate these boundaries, they undermine their spiritual authority and harm those they are entrusted to lead.

Servant leadership—leadership rooted in humility and service to others—is the solution to many of the problems facing the church today. Many leaders have lost their integrity, spirituality, and faith in God. They lead not with humility, but with pride. Servant leadership calls us to influence others toward their God-given purpose, not to exploit our authority for personal gain.

The church is facing a crisis of leadership, particularly in the area of sexual integrity. Leaders must rise to the standard God has set for them, and the church must hold them accountable with love and grace. Servant leadership offers a path forward—a way to lead with integrity, transparency, and humility. As the church addresses these issues, it must also prepare the next generation to live lives that honor God's design for sexuality and leadership.

Reflection | Action | Prayer

This reflection calls you to examine the impact of public perception and personal accountability within the church. How do your actions, and the actions of leaders, affect how the church is seen by others?

Through the questions, consider how you can live with humility and transparency, becoming a true witness of Christ's love.

Use the action steps to engage in deeper self-examination, and close with a prayer, asking for grace to live with integrity in the eyes of both God and the world.

Reflection Questions:

1. Am I honest about my struggles with others, or do I hide behind a mask of perfection?

2. How has pride played a role in my life, and what steps can I take to humble myself before God?

3. In what ways can I reflect God's love and grace in public, especially regarding sensitive topics like sexuality?

Future Action Steps:

- Identify any areas of pride or hidden struggles and commit to bringing them before God in humility.

- Reflect on James 4:6 and pray for the humility to confront sin in your life and ask for God's help.

- Take time to listen to others' struggles without judgment, offering grace and support as Christ would.

A Prayer for Humility and Integrity in Public Witness

Father, I ask for Your guidance in helping me live a life of transparency and integrity before others. Help me to walk in humility, knowing that pride leads to destruction (Proverbs 16:18).

May I be a faithful ambassador of Christ, representing You with truth and love in every area of my life (2 Corinthians 5:20).

Where I have fallen short, I ask for Your forgiveness, and I trust in Your promise to cleanse me from all unrighteousness (1 John 1:9).

Give me the strength to be a light to those around me and to handle delicate issues with grace and wisdom. In Jesus' name, Amen.

Chapter 4
WHAT ARE WE AS LEADERS DOING ABOUT THE ISSUE?

> *"True leadership in the church begins with humility, accountability, and a commitment to live above reproach. Restoration and integrity must be the foundation of our calling."*

As leaders, we are called to meet people where they are—both inside and outside the church. Our role requires us to be blameless, avoiding behaviors that do not align with the will of God. We must embody the love of Jesus Christ, extending that love to everyone, whether they are rich or poor, young or old, healthy or sick. In many cases, we are the only representation of Christ that some people may ever see.

Sexual sin is unique in that it directly violates the body, which the Bible tells us is the temple of the Holy Spirit. *"You are not your own; you were bought at a price. Therefore, honor God with your bodies"* (1 Corinthians 6:19-20 NIV). We are not to defile this temple through sexual sin, and yet, it is rampant, even among leaders. The Bible offers numerous warnings about sexual immorality (Proverbs 6:32, Ephesians 5:3, Galatians 5:19, 1 Thessalonians 4:3). However, God also promises that we will not be tempted beyond what we can bear, providing a way of escape for us (1 Corinthians 10:13).

Jesus calls us to control our bodies in holiness and honor, not in the passion of lust like those who do not know God. *"Let all that you do be done in love"* (1 Corinthians 16:14 ESV). Yet many leaders are falling short of this standard, succumbing to temptations that damage their witness and the church.

The Call to Covenant and Faithfulness

From the beginning, God has called us into a covenant relationship with Him. This relationship is based on love and faithfulness. Throughout history, God reached out to His people through prophets, priests, kings, despised women, and even nameless slaves. In Romans 10:14-15, Paul writes: *"How then shall they call on Him in whom they have not believed? And how shall they believe in Him of whom they have not heard? And how shall they hear without a preacher?"* As leaders, we must seek God for guidance and remain free from the entanglements of sin.

Yet, despite this high calling, we see leaders engaging in casual sex and other forms of sexual immorality. Shockingly, a significant number of Christians, including 62% of Catholics and 54% of Protestants, believe that casual sex is acceptable as long as it is consensual. The concept of chastity, once a cornerstone of Christian teaching, has become almost obsolete.

Jesus' command to love God with all our heart, soul, and mind (Matthew 22:37-40) is foundational, yet we are failing to live it out. We are focused on what we want, neglecting the true work of the church, which is to love, serve, and proclaim the gospel.

The Early Church: Lessons for Today

The early Christian church faced many challenges, including societal opposition and internal strife. Despite being a minority, early Christians spread their message with boldness and conviction. They were not focused on their own needs but on advancing God's kingdom. Slaves, despised members of society, found spiritual equality within the Christian community, and the power of the Holy Spirit was evident in the lives of believers.

Today, the church faces similar challenges, but many leaders have lost focus. Some pastors are hired for their ability to speak well, but lack the spiritual depth, holy living, and commitment to lead effectively. They preach everything but the word of God, and the result is a church that resembles the world more than it reflects the kingdom of God.

Paul warned of this in 2 Timothy 4:3-4: *"For the time will come when they will not endure sound doctrine; but after their own lusts shall they heap to themselves teachers, having itching ears; and they shall turn away their ears from the truth, and shall be turned unto fables."*

Our forefathers labored in the word, preaching the unadulterated gospel of Jesus Christ. But now, false teachers and prophets are leading people astray. The Bible tells us in Matthew 24:24 ESV that *"false Christs and false prophets will arise and perform great signs and wonders, so as to lead astray, if possible, even the elect."*

Leaders and the Misuse of Scripture

Today, many leaders misuse the Bible. They engage in *eisegesis*—reading into the text what they want it to mean—rather than *exegesis*, which is the process of drawing out the text's true meaning. Bible studies often focus on personal interpretations, asking, *"What does this text mean to you?"* rather than seeking the true meaning of Scripture. This approach weakens the church, leading to a faith that is shallow and ineffective.

Leaders have also become less interested in Bible study, focusing instead on tithes, offerings, and attendance numbers. The church is more concerned with keeping the lights on than with the spiritual health of the community. Baptism and the Lord's Supper have been neglected, and faith has become a hollow word with little meaning.

Returning to the Basics: What Is Our Role as Leaders?

If we want to see revival in the church, we must return to the basics. We must remember our role as leaders and the high calling we have received from God.

1. ***Love as Jesus Loved:*** Jesus called us to love one another, but we cannot give what we do not have. *"Hurt people hurt people,"* and many leaders are leading from a place of brokenness. We must first learn to love ourselves through the healing power of God's word before we can love others effectively.

2. ***Care for the Lost:*** The church has become a social network, a place where we are more focused on filling seats than on filling souls with the truth of the gospel. We no longer knock on doors to share the good news. Instead, we wait for visitors to come to us and hope they'll fill out a card. But people want to know how much we care, not how much we know.

3. ***Return to Prayer:*** We no longer pray as we used to, except to tell God what we want. When was the last time we asked Him what He wants? Prayer is the foundation of our relationship with God and the key to fulfilling the church's mission.

4. ***Reignite Our Passion for Christ:*** We claim to have a passion for Jesus, but do we have His compassion for others? The church has been commissioned to serve, and we must return to that calling with urgency and commitment.

The 21st Century Church: A Watchman's Call

As the church continues to change with the times, many Christians are asking, *"Where can I find a church with uncompromising, biblical teaching?"* Churches are increasingly replacing the power of the Holy Spirit with emotional manipulation through loud music, presentations, and programs that mimic the world. But God is asking, *"Where am I in all of this?"*

Each of us is called to be a watchman, not just the pastors and ministry leaders. We are all laborers in the vineyard, responsible for holding one another accountable. When we see something out of order in the church, it is our duty to speak up.

What are we, as leaders, doing about the issues facing the church today? It's time to return to the basics—to love, to serve, to pray, and to lead with integrity. The church's mission is not to entertain but to transform lives through the power of the gospel. Leaders, let us rise to the call and give the world something real—a faith rooted in Christ and lived out with compassion, truth, and love.

Reflection | Action | Prayer

This section is aimed at those in leadership or those aspiring to lead. You'll be encouraged to take a hard look at your leadership style, integrity, and areas where you may need to improve.

The reflection questions will help you identify places where growth is needed, and the action steps will guide you in seeking accountability and humility in your role. End by praying for God's wisdom and strength as you lead with integrity and love.

Reflection Questions:

1. As a leader (or aspiring leader), am I leading with integrity, or are there areas where I am falling short?

_____
_____
_____
_____
_____
_____
_____

2. How can I exemplify the love of Christ to those who look up to me in leadership?

3. What areas in my spiritual walk need strengthening so I can better lead others?

Future Action Steps:

- Ask God to reveal areas in your life or leadership where you may need to grow.
- Read 1 Timothy 3:1-7 to understand the qualities of a good leader and assess how you can live up to them.
- Set up an accountability relationship with a fellow leader or trusted person in your life.

A Prayer for Wisdom and Accountability in Leadership

Lord, as a leader, I ask You to give me the wisdom and strength to shepherd Your people with integrity, as instructed in 1 Timothy 3:1-7. Help me to live above reproach and to lead by example, demonstrating the love and grace of Christ.

If I have failed in any area, I ask for Your forgiveness, knowing that You restore the humble and contrite in spirit (Isaiah 57:15).

Guide me to be accountable and transparent, always pointing others toward You. Help me to reflect Your holiness in my life and leadership, for Your glory. In Jesus' name, Amen.

Chapter 5
DISCIPLESHIP FOR THE UNCHURCHED

"Reaching the unchurched requires authenticity, humility, and a heart committed to discipleship. The church's mission is not just to welcome people but to guide them into a transformative relationship with Christ."

One of the most common questions Christians ask others is, *"Are you saved?"* Often, the answer is a quick yes, even when the individual may have a completely misguided understanding of salvation. Another frequent question is, *"Do you know the Lord?"* Again, many people answer yes while holding erroneous views of who Jesus truly is.

Jesus, however, asked His disciples a far deeper question: *"Who do you say that I am?"* Peter's response did not come from human wisdom but from the Holy Spirit. His answer—*"You are the Christ, the Son of the living God"*—revealed that Peter had been drawn by the Father and taught by Him (Matthew 16:16 ESV).

This response showed that Peter had received true revelation, the foundation of salvation. For leaders, understanding this distinction is crucial as we engage with the unchurched and those who profess faith without fully grasping its meaning.

Breaking Down Barriers Between the Church & the Unchurched

Leaders today often carry titles and degrees that unintentionally create barriers between them and the unchurched. People without a church background may feel intimidated or unsure of how to approach us. They are not interested in hearing about our accolades or theological accomplishments. What they are looking for is transparency—authenticity that shows we, too, are human and face struggles.

Being a Christian does not mean we have it all together. Leaders, like everyone else, face challenges in their marriages, families, and personal lives. The unchurched are seeking leaders who are willing to be honest about their struggles. *"We all have sinned and come short of the glory of God"* (Romans 3:23 NKJV). By remaining transparent and resisting the urge to chase after trends, we can connect with the unchurched on a deeper level. Authenticity is what non-believers expect from us.

Discipleship in a Fast-Paced World

Discipleship in the 21st-century church can be difficult because of our "microwave mentality"—we want everything to happen quickly. But spiritual growth takes time and dedication. Too often, we rush new members, pushing them before they are ready. When this happens, they leave the church unprepared, sometimes returning to the world or joining another church without ever being truly discipled.

Leaders must ask themselves: *Is our church ready for future disciples?* We may want to reach more people, but so much has changed in how we engage with the world today. The mission God gave the early disciples remains the same today: *"Go and make disciples of all nations"* (Matthew 28:19 NIV). But many leaders don't feel successful in this mission. Some churches have the wrong people in key positions, which hinders growth. People are leading praise and worship, teaching Sunday school, and ushering, yet they won't attend prayer meetings. How can we expect to be effective leaders when we don't submit to the basic requirements of the church?

Addressing Sin and Restoring the Church

In the early church, sin was confronted and dealt with directly. In the Garden of Eden, pride was the root of Adam and Eve's fall, and that same pride continues to lead people into sin today. Leaders often fall into immoral behavior because pride convinces them that sinful pleasure is worth the risk. But this is spiritual blindness.

The Apostle Paul addressed sexual sin in the church at Corinth, calling out their tolerance of immoral behavior. Similarly, we cannot disregard sin in our churches today. The goal is not to shame individuals but to restore them to their rightful place so the church can move forward in a positive direction (Galatians 6:1). Confession and repentance are necessary before true restoration can occur.

Preparing for Growth

Churches should be focused on growing into healthy, Christ-like environments where people love God and one another. However, growth is often stunted because the wrong people are in leadership roles. Some churches are stagnant—no one is coming, and those who are there are not growing. Leaders need to prioritize reaching those who have never heard the gospel or who have left the church disillusioned.

Are we prepared for the influx of new members God will bring? Do we have our praise and worship team in place? Are our ushers trained to handle the flow of people who will fill our altars? Leaders in the 21st-century church must prepare themselves for growth, keeping their hearts and minds focused on God's mission.

A Time of Urgency: Are We Ready?

We are living in a time where people are asking, *"Are we in the end times?"* The pandemic has awakened a sense of urgency in many, prompting questions about the signs of the times. As fear grips the hearts of many, the church must be ready to provide answers rooted in God's Word.

God will add to the church in His timing. *"The Lord added to the church daily those who were being saved"* (Acts 2:47 NKJV). Are we, as leaders, prepared for this growth? Are we equipping ourselves and our churches to handle the revival that is coming?

Feeding Our Spirits

As leaders, we must feed our spirits with God's Word, especially when it comes to addressing sin. *"Finally, brethren, whatever is true, whatever is honorable, whatever is just, whatever is pure, whatever is lovely, whatever is commendable, if there is any excellence, if there is anything worthy of praise, think about these things"* (Philippians 4:8 ESV).

Jesus set the example for how to combat temptation, using Scripture to remind the devil of the truth: *"Man shall not live by bread alone, but by every word that comes from the mouth of God"* (Matthew 4:4 ESV). We, too, must remind ourselves of who we are and whose we are. God is our refuge, a very present help in trouble.

Bringing Glory to God Through Obedience

We were created to bring glory to God, and one of the ways we do that is by living in obedience to His will. Obedience is not just about avoiding sinful behavior; it's about staying focused on what matters—bringing hope to others. When we live lives that reflect God's love and surrender to His will, we glorify Him in all we do.

Discipleship is not a quick process, but it is essential to the growth and health of the church. As leaders, we must be transparent, patient, and committed to preparing ourselves and our churches for the revival God is bringing. By staying focused on God's mission, feeding our spirits, and living lives of obedience, we can bring glory to God and fulfill the call to make disciples.

Reflection | Action | Prayer

In this reflection, you will think about your role in reaching those who are unchurched or unfamiliar with the gospel. The questions will encourage you to reflect on how you can be a more effective disciple-maker, connecting with others in authentic ways.

As you move through the action steps, consider how you can mentor others and be a light in your community. Close this reflection with a prayer, asking God to help you fulfill the Great Commission and lead others into a deeper relationship with Him.

Reflection Questions:

1. How can I better connect with those who are unchurched or unfamiliar with the gospel?

2. What are some ways I can be more transparent and authentic in my relationships with others?

3. Am I actively involved in discipleship, helping others grow in their faith?

Future Action Steps:

- Take a step toward mentoring someone or inviting an unchurched friend to a service or Bible study.
- Reflect on Matthew 28:19 and ask God to show you how to make disciples in your community.
- Be intentional about having real, honest conversations with those around you about faith and struggles.

A Prayer for Boldness & Compassion in Reaching the Unchurched

Father, I ask for Your help in reaching those who are far from You, as You have called us to be fishers of men (Matthew 4:19). May I always be transparent and authentic in my relationships, reflecting the love of Christ to the unchurched. Let my words and actions be a witness to Your grace and truth.

Give me the courage to fulfill the Great Commission, teaching others to observe all that You have commanded (Matthew 28:20). Help me to be patient and diligent as I disciple others, knowing that You are the one who brings the increase (1 Corinthians 3:6). In Jesus' name, Amen.

Chapter 6
WAYS TO OVERCOME SEXUAL SIN

"Freedom from sexual sin begins with bringing hidden struggles into the light, renewing your mind with God's Word, and walking daily in the power of the Holy Spirit."

Sexual sin can be a persistent and powerful struggle, but through the power of God, we can overcome it. The following steps outline practical ways to break free from the grip of sexual sin and live in the righteousness that God has called us to.

1. *Know Who You Are: Your Identity in Christ*

Many people base their identity on their sexuality, believing that fulfillment is found through sexual expression. But as children of God, our identity is rooted in Christ, not in our desires. We must understand who we are in Him—beloved, redeemed, and made new. *"Therefore, if anyone is in Christ, the new creation has come: The old has gone, the new is here!"* (2 Corinthians 5:17 NIV).

2. Walk in the Light and Confess Your Sins

We are children of God, and sexual sin has no power over us unless we give it power. *"If we confess our sins, He is faithful and just to forgive us our sins and to cleanse us from all unrighteousness"* (1 John 1:9 NKJV). By confessing our sins to one another and to God, we bring the sin into the light, where it loses its grip on us. Healing begins when we expose the sin, no longer allowing it to hold us in bondage.

3. Break the Cycle by Exposing the Sin

When we keep our sexual sin hidden, it gains power over us. Fear of failure, rejection, or loss keeps us trapped in the cycle of secrecy. However, once we bring the sin to light, it loses its power, and healing can begin. Shame and fear are tools the enemy uses to keep us bound, but freedom comes through confession and repentance.

4. Change Your Way of Thinking

We are not who we once were. God has given us a new mind and a new way of thinking. Ephesians 4:22-24 NIV tells us, *"Put off your old self, which is being corrupted by its deceitful desires; be made new in the attitude of your minds; and put on the new self, created to be like God in true righteousness and holiness."* As new creatures in Christ, we must shift our focus from sin to God, allowing His Word to renew our minds and transform our behavior.

5. Flee from Sexual Sin

1 Corinthians 6:18-20 NIV commands us to flee from sexual immorality: *"Flee from sexual immorality. All other sins a person commits are outside the body, but whoever sins sexually sins against their own body."* To flee means to run—to run to Jesus in prayer, to run to His Word, and to avoid situations that may lead to temptation. This is an active decision to remove ourselves from anything that may cause us to stumble.

Redemption from Sexual Sin

Sexual sin can often feel like a cycle that's hard to break, but redemption is always possible through Jesus Christ. Some may struggle with misconceptions about who Jesus is and what He can do. Reading Ephesians 4 can help guide us in how we are to live and conduct ourselves as followers of Christ.

Developing an Adult Discipleship Plan

Churches must create a Basic Discipleship Course to help new believers and the unchurched grow in their faith. Once trust is established between the individual and the church, leaders can implement this course to teach them what it means to be part of a faith community.

Potential topics could include:

1. Heeding the Call
2. Prayer: The Key to Growth
3. Witnessing
4. Jesus Christ: The Son of God
5. Jesus Christ: The Son of Man
6. What Does It Mean to Be a Disciple?
7. The Great Commission
8. What Does Spiritual Maturity Look Like?
9. Building Trust in Leadership
10. What Is Faith?

Leaders' Role in Evangelism and Discipleship

God is holy, and He is always working to reconcile His church back to Himself. As leaders, we must be ready to roll up our sleeves, help people pray through their struggles, and find peace in a chaotic world. In times like these, the church may be the only place of refuge for many. Are we, as leaders, prepared for the influx of people seeking hope and healing?

Our churches must be ready for evangelism and discipleship. Leaders need to be in their rightful place, guiding the church forward with integrity and dedication to the mission of Christ.

Lord, I thank You for the freedom You have given me through Christ. As Your Word tells me to flee from sexual immorality (1 Corinthians 6:18), I ask for Your strength to resist temptation and walk in the newness of life You have provided. Help me to renew my mind daily by Your Word, as Ephesians 4:22-24 instructs, putting off the old self and putting on the new self, created to be like You in true righteousness and holiness. May I always be mindful of Your presence, knowing that I am a temple of the Holy Spirit (1 Corinthians 6:19). In Jesus' name, Amen.

Reflection | Action | Prayer

This reflection is designed to help you identify and break free from areas of sexual sin or temptation. The questions will prompt you to think about your identity in Christ and areas where you need to bring sin into the light.

Through the action steps, you will be guided to make practical changes and rely on God's Word to renew your mind. Finish with a prayer for deliverance and strength, asking God to help you walk in freedom and holiness.

Reflection Questions:

1. Are there areas of sexual sin in my life that I need to bring into the light and confess?

2. Do I know my true identity in Christ, or am I allowing other things to define me?

How can I take practical steps to flee from temptation and renew my mind?

Future Action Steps:

- Confess any hidden sin to a trusted person or spiritual leader, and ask for accountability.

- Study Ephesians 4 and meditate on verses 22-24, asking God to renew your mind and help you put on the new self.

- Create a plan for avoiding situations that lead to temptation, and replace them with time spent in prayer and Scripture.

A Prayer for Deliverance and Renewal of the Mind

Heavenly Father, I come before You with a humble heart, confessing the struggles I have faced and the sins that have entangled me. I ask for Your forgiveness and grace to cover me. Lord, I acknowledge that I cannot overcome these struggles in my own strength, but I believe in Your power to deliver me. Your Word says that if we confess our sins, You are faithful and just to forgive us and to cleanse us from all unrighteousness (1 John 1:9). Cleanse my heart and mind, Lord, and make me new.

Father, I renounce every sinful desire and every foothold the enemy has gained in my life. I ask You to break every chain of sexual sin, lust, and impurity that has bound me. I claim the freedom that is mine through the blood of Jesus Christ, for Your Word declares, "If the Son sets you free, you will be free indeed" (John 8:36). Fill me with the Holy Spirit so that I may walk in the power and authority You have given me.

Help me to flee from temptation, Lord, just as Joseph fled from sin (Genesis 39:12). Teach me to take every thought captive and make it obedient to Christ, as Your Word instructs in 2 Corinthians 10:5. Guard my mind and heart, Father, and replace every lie of the enemy with the truth of Your Word. I reject thoughts of shame, guilt, unworthiness, and defeat. I declare that I am a new creation in Christ; the old has gone, and the new has come (2 Corinthians 5:17).

Restoring Integrity and Rebuilding Trust in Church Leadership

Lord, I ask You to renew my mind daily with Your Word and transform my thinking to align with Your will (Romans 12:2). Create in me a clean heart, O God, and renew a steadfast spirit within me (Psalm 51:10). Teach me to meditate on things that are true, noble, right, pure, lovely, and admirable (Philippians 4:8). Help me to dwell on Your goodness and faithfulness instead of the lies of the enemy.

Father, I surrender every part of my life to You—my thoughts, my actions, my desires, and my relationships. Lead me on the path of righteousness for Your name's sake (Psalm 23:3). Surround me with godly influences and accountability partners who will encourage and support me in my walk of faith.

Lord, I thank You for Your unending mercy and love. You have promised never to leave me or forsake me (Deuteronomy 31:6). Walk with me daily as I strive to live a life that honors and glorifies You. Strengthen me to persevere in moments of weakness, and remind me that through Christ, I am more than a conqueror (Romans 8:37).

I declare that I am free, I am forgiven, and I am made whole by Your grace. Thank You for the victory that is already mine in Jesus Christ. I commit my life into Your hands and trust You to lead me in the way everlasting. In the mighty name of Jesus, I pray. Amen.

Chapter 7
BREAKING FREE THROUGH CHRIST

"Deliverance is a journey, not a one-time event. Through repentance, renewal, and reliance on the Holy Spirit, we walk in the freedom and authority Christ has given us."

Prayers for Deliverance and Repentance

Deliverance is not a one-time event; it's a process, a journey toward complete freedom in Christ. Whether you are battling a demonic stronghold, a mental stronghold, or habitual sin, the power of the Holy Spirit is available to set you free. Jesus came that we might have life, and have it abundantly (John 10:10). As believers, we are not meant to live in bondage, but to walk in the freedom and authority Christ has given us.

This section will guide you through prayers of repentance and deliverance, helping you confront any spiritual or mental strongholds that may be keeping you from living fully in God's truth.

A Prayer of Repentance: Returning to God's Grace

Before seeking deliverance, we must first come before God in humility, confessing our sins and turning away from anything that has separated us from His will. Repentance is the first step to freedom, and it opens the door for God's healing power to flow through our lives. It is not simply an admission of wrongdoing, but a heartfelt desire to be restored to right standing with God and to walk in the fullness of His purpose for our lives.

***Prayer of Repentance:** Heavenly Father, I come before You today with a humble heart, acknowledging that I have fallen short of Your glory (Romans 3:23). I confess my sins to You—both those I am aware of and those I may not even recognize. I repent of my actions, thoughts, attitudes, and behaviors that have grieved Your heart and led me away from Your perfect will. I am sorry, Lord, for the times I have chosen my own way over Yours.*

I ask for Your forgiveness and grace to wash over me, as Your Word promises that if we confess our sins, You are faithful and just to forgive us and cleanse us from all unrighteousness (1 John 1:9). Lord, I renounce every sin I have committed, every thought or action that has kept me in bondage, and I turn away from those things now. Teach me to hate the things that grieve You and to love what pleases You.

Restoring Integrity and Rebuilding Trust in Church Leadership

Cleanse me, Lord, and renew a right spirit within me (Psalm 51:10). Restore to me the joy of Your salvation and uphold me with a willing spirit. Fill the empty spaces in my heart with Your presence so that I no longer seek fulfillment in things that are not of You. I thank You for the blood of Jesus that cleanses me, redeems me, and sets me free. Thank You for calling me back into Your loving arms.

Father, I commit my life to You again. I surrender every area of my life—my thoughts, desires, actions, and plans. Align my will with Yours, and guide me in the path of righteousness for Your name's sake (Psalm 23:3). Help me to walk forward in obedience and humility, fully devoted to You and Your purpose for my life. Thank You for Your love, mercy, and faithfulness that never fail.

In the name of Jesus Christ, I pray. Amen.

Breaking Free from Demonic Strongholds

If there are areas in your life where you feel there is a demonic hold—whether it's through addiction, persistent sinful habits, or a pattern of thoughts that lead you away from God—this prayer is for you. Jesus has given us authority over all the power of the enemy (Luke 10:19), and through His name, we can command any spirit that opposes His will to leave. Deliverance is a declaration of freedom through Christ, breaking every chain that binds us and reclaiming our identity as children of God.

Prayer of Deliverance from Demonic Strongholds: *In the mighty name of Jesus Christ, I come before You, Father, and take authority over every demonic spirit that has taken hold of my life. Your Word declares that You have given me power to tread on serpents and scorpions and over all the power of the enemy, and nothing shall by any means harm me (Luke 10:19). By the authority of Christ, I bind every spirit of lust, pride, sexual immorality, fear, addiction, rebellion, anxiety, and any spirit that opposes the will of God in my life.*

I break every stronghold and generational curse that has kept me bound in sin. I reject every lie that the enemy has spoken over me, and I renounce every agreement I have knowingly or unknowingly made with the kingdom of darkness. In the name of Jesus, I declare that every unclean spirit must leave me now. You have no power over me, for I have been redeemed by the blood of Jesus Christ (Colossians 1:13-14), and I belong to God. I cancel every plan, plot, and scheme of the enemy that has been set against my life, and I call it null and void in the name of Jesus.

Father, I ask You to fill every empty space in my heart with Your Holy Spirit. Cleanse me from all unrighteousness and fill me with Your love, peace, and joy. Let no room remain for darkness, and surround me with Your presence and protection. Let Your Word be a lamp to my feet and a light to my path (Psalm 119:105), guiding me as I walk in freedom.

I declare my freedom in Christ, for Your Word says, "Whom the Son sets free is free indeed" (John 8:36). I stand on the promises of God that no weapon formed against me shall prosper (Isaiah 54:17). I reject all fear, for You have not given me a spirit of fear, but of power, love, and a sound mind (2 Timothy 1:7). Lord, strengthen me to walk in the authority You have given me, and help me to resist the enemy so that he will flee from me (James 4:7).

Thank You, Father, for the victory that is already mine in Christ Jesus. I praise You for delivering me and for setting me free. I commit my life to You, and I will walk in the light of Your truth all the days of my life. In the mighty and matchless name of Jesus Christ, I pray. Amen.

Overcoming Mental Strongholds

Mental strongholds—patterns of thinking that keep us in cycles of doubt, fear, shame, or insecurity—can be just as powerful as demonic strongholds. They affect how we see ourselves, how we relate to God, and how we navigate life. These strongholds often stem from lies the enemy plants in our hearts or from past wounds that shape our self-perception. But God has given us the tools to tear them down. His Word tells us to *"take every thought captive to make it obedient to Christ"* (2 Corinthians 10:5 NIV). By replacing lies with the truth of God's Word, we can renew our minds and walk in the freedom and confidence that comes from knowing who we are in Christ.

Prayer to Break Mental Strongholds: *Father God, I come before You today, surrendering my mind and thoughts to Your authority. I acknowledge that I have allowed negative thoughts, lies, and doubts to take root in my heart. These patterns of thinking have kept me in cycles of fear, insecurity, shame, and unworthiness, and I repent for believing these lies instead of trusting in Your truth. Lord, forgive me for any area where I have doubted Your love and promises.*

Your Word says that You have not given me a spirit of fear, but of power, love, and a sound mind (2 Timothy 1:7). I claim that sound mind today, and I ask You to renew my thoughts with the power of Your Word. I take every thought captive and make it obedient to Christ (2 Corinthians 10:5).

I reject every thought that does not align with Your truth. I reject fear, guilt, shame, doubt, and insecurity. I reject the lies that say I am unworthy, unloved, or incapable. Instead, I declare that I am who You say I am—loved, forgiven, redeemed, and set free (Ephesians 1:7). I am fearfully and wonderfully made, created in Your image, and called for a purpose (Psalm 139:14).

Lord, help me to meditate on Your Word day and night so that I may be transformed by the renewing of my mind (Romans 12:2). Teach me to think on things that are true, noble, right, pure, lovely, and admirable (Philippians 4:8). Fill my mind with thoughts of hope, joy, and peace that come from trusting in You. Replace every lie with Your truth, and every doubt with faith. Let Your truth be my foundation and my guide.

Father, I ask that You break every mental stronghold that has held me captive. Heal the wounds in my heart that gave these thoughts a foothold in my life. Where there has been fear, give me courage. Where there has been doubt, give me confidence. Where there has been shame, give me the assurance of Your love and grace. Strengthen me to stand firm against the enemy's schemes, knowing that I have the mind of Christ (1 Corinthians 2:16).

Thank You, Lord, for the power of Your Word and the freedom You have given me through Jesus Christ. I will walk forward in the knowledge of who I am in You and live according to Your will. In the name of Jesus, I pray. Amen.

Prayer for Protection and Strength

After experiencing deliverance, it's important to stay grounded in God's Word and His presence. The enemy will often attempt to bring temptation, discouragement, or spiritual attack, but the power of the Holy Spirit equips us to stand firm. God's promise to protect and sustain us is a source of hope and confidence as we continue walking in healing and restoration. This prayer invites God's protection and strength as you persevere in your faith journey.

Prayer for Protection and Strength: *Heavenly Father, I come before You with a heart full of gratitude for the deliverance and freedom You have given me. Thank You for breaking the chains that once held me and for setting me on a path of healing and restoration. You are my refuge and my fortress, my God in whom I trust (Psalm 91:2). I ask for Your continued divine protection as I walk this journey of faith.*

Lord, I know the enemy will try to tempt me and draw me back into old ways, but I declare today that greater is He who is in me than he who is in the world (1 John 4:4). Strengthen me with Your Spirit, Lord, so that I can resist every scheme of the enemy. Help me to stand firm in the truth of Your Word and to walk in the freedom You have given me.

Cover me with Your full armor so that I may be able to withstand the attacks of the enemy. Gird me with the belt of truth, protect my heart with the breastplate of righteousness, and prepare my feet with the gospel of peace. Strengthen my faith to wield the shield of faith, quenching every fiery dart of the enemy. Guard my mind with the helmet of salvation and arm me with the sword of the Spirit, which is Your Word (Ephesians 6:10-17). I put on this armor daily, knowing that it is Your power that equips me to stand.

Let no weapon formed against me prosper, Lord (Isaiah 54:17). Guard my mind from lies, my heart from fear, and my spirit from discouragement. Help me to remain steadfast, unmovable, and always abounding in Your work (1 Corinthians 15:58). Fill me with Your peace that surpasses all understanding, guarding my heart and mind in Christ Jesus (Philippians 4:7).

Lord, keep my eyes fixed on You, the Author and Finisher of my faith (Hebrews 12:2). Guide me in Your truth and teach me to hear Your voice above all others. Surround me with Your presence and remind me daily that You are my shield and my defender. May Your promises be my anchor and Your Spirit my strength as I continue to grow in my faith and trust in You.

Father, I thank You for Your faithfulness and for Your unfailing love. You are my hiding place and my strong tower. I declare that my life is in Your hands, and no power of darkness can snatch me from Your care. Thank You for walking with me every step of the way and for giving me victory through Jesus Christ. In His name, I pray. Amen.

Prayer for Healing and Wholeness

Deliverance is more than just freedom from sin or bondage—it's a journey toward healing and wholeness. God desires to restore every part of your life and bring you to a place of peace, joy, and completeness in Him. Healing goes beyond the surface; it penetrates the deep wounds, past hurts, and emotional scars, allowing you to walk in the fullness of God's plan for your life. This prayer invites God's restorative power to touch every area of your being—spiritually, emotionally, and physically.

Prayer for Healing and Wholeness: *Lord Jesus, I come before You as my Healer and my Redeemer. I thank You for Your love that never fails and for Your grace that sustains me. I ask You now to bring healing to every wounded place in my life. Heal the deep wounds of my past and the scars left by sin and hurt. Where there has been brokenness, Lord, I ask You to bring wholeness. Where there has been rejection, let me feel the embrace of Your acceptance. Where there has been fear, let Your perfect love cast it out (1 John 4:18).*

Father, I bring before You the pain, disappointment, and bitterness that may have taken root in my heart. I ask You to help me release these burdens to You, knowing that You care for me (1 Peter 5:7). Teach me to forgive those who have wronged me, even when it feels impossible. Just as You have forgiven me, Lord, I choose to forgive. I release every grudge, every hurt, and every offense, and I ask that You replace them with Your peace and love.

Lord, restore my soul. Rebuild the areas of my life that have been torn down by sin, failure, and pain. You are the One who makes all things new (Revelation 21:5). Fill every empty space in my heart with Your Spirit and every broken place with Your healing touch. Help me to see myself as You see me—loved, valued, and redeemed. Remind me daily that I am fearfully and wonderfully made in Your image (Psalm 139:14).

Father, I ask for healing not only in my spirit but also in my emotions and my body. Where there has been anxiety, bring peace. Where there has been despair, fill me with hope. Where there has been physical pain or illness, bring Your healing power, for by Your stripes, I am healed (Isaiah 53:5). Let Your joy be my strength and Your peace rule my heart and mind (Nehemiah 8:10, Colossians 3:15).

Guide me, Lord, into the fullness of life that You have promised. Help me to walk daily in Your love and grace, knowing that You are with me every step of the way. Thank You for being my refuge, my strength, and my Healer. I place my trust in You, confident that You will complete the good work You have begun in me (Philippians 1:6).

I declare today that I am whole, healed, and restored by the power of Your love. Thank You, Lord, for the freedom and healing You have brought into my life. I will continue to seek

You and trust You, knowing that You are faithful. In the mighty name of Jesus, I pray. Amen.

A Final Declaration of Freedom

This final declaration is meant to affirm your freedom in Christ and serve as a powerful reminder of the victory that is already yours. Speak these words boldly, proclaiming the truth of who you are in Christ. Let it be a declaration of faith, a testimony of deliverance, and a commitment to live in the power and authority of Jesus Christ. You are no longer bound by sin, fear, or shame—you are free indeed!

Declaration of Freedom: *I declare that I am free in the name of Jesus. I have been redeemed by the blood of the Lamb, and I am no longer bound by sin, shame, or fear (Revelation 12:11). I am a new creation in Christ; the old has gone, and the new has come (2 Corinthians 5:17). No stronghold has power over me, for I have been set free by the truth of God's Word (John 8:32).*

No chain can bind me, no lie can deceive me, and no weapon formed against me shall prosper (Isaiah 54:17). I reject every plan of the enemy and cancel every assignment against my life in the name of Jesus. I take authority over every spirit that opposes the will of God, and I command it to leave my life completely. I declare that my mind is renewed, my heart is restored, and my spirit is strengthened through Christ.

I am no longer a slave to sin, for I have been adopted into the family of God as His beloved child (Romans 8:15). I have been chosen and called for His purpose (1 Peter 2:9), and I will live as a reflection of His grace, love, and power. My life belongs to the Lord, and I will walk in the freedom of the Holy Spirit, fulfilling the good plans He has prepared for me (Jeremiah 29:11).

I declare that every generational curse is broken, every stronghold has been torn down, and every chain has been destroyed by the name and power of Jesus Christ. I will live in the abundant life that Jesus came to give me (John 10:10). I will not be moved by fear or doubt, but I will stand firm in the promises of God, knowing that I am more than a conqueror through Christ who loves me (Romans 8:37).

Father, I thank You for the victory that is mine through Your Son. I will walk boldly in the freedom You have given me, bringing glory to Your name in all that I do. My testimony will be a light to others, showing them that the same God who delivered me can deliver them as well. I am free indeed, and I will live as a witness to Your power and goodness. In the mighty and matchless name of Jesus, I declare this truth. Amen.

Deliverance is a Journey
It is a process of transformation that leads to true freedom, lasting peace, and complete restoration.

As you continue to walk with Christ, remember that each step brings you closer to the fullness of life He has promised. Keep these prayers close to your heart, allowing them to guide and strengthen you as you lean on the Holy Spirit.

Be encouraged that God is faithful to complete the good work He has begun in you (Philippians 1:6). Trust in His timing, His power, and His unwavering love for you. No matter how challenging the path may seem, you are not walking it alone. He goes before you, stands beside you, and surrounds you with His grace. Rest in the assurance that His presence will sustain you every step of the way.

The journey of deliverance is not just about freedom from sin; it's about embracing the abundant life that Jesus has secured for you. Walk boldly in His truth, knowing that you are loved, chosen, and redeemed. With God, restoration is not only possible—it is certain.

Made in the USA
Columbia, SC
28 April 2025